BROADWAY FAVORITES

Solos and String Orchestra Arrangements
Correlated with Essential Elements String Method

Arranged by
LLOYD CONLEY

Welcome to Essential Elements Broadway Favorites! There are two versions of each selection in this versatile book. The SOLO version appears in the beginning of your book. The STRING ORCHESTRA arrangements of each song follows. The supplemental CD recording or string orchestra PIANO PART may be used as an accompaniment for solo performance. Use these recordings when playing solos for friends and family.

Solo Page	String Arr. Page	Title	Correlated with Essential Elements
3	14/15	Edelweiss	Book 1, page 34
4	16/17	Beauty And The Beast	Book 1, page 42
5	18/19	Circle Of Life	Book 1, page 42
6	20/21	I Dreamed A Dream	Book 2, page 30
7	22/23	The Phantom Of The Opera	Book 2, page 30
8	24/25	Sun And Moon	Book 2, page 30
9	26/27	Cabaret	Book 2, page 43
10	28/29	Get Me To The Church On Time	Book 2, page 43
11	30/31	Go Go Go Joseph	Book 2, page 43
12	32/33	Memory	Book 2, page 43
13	34/35	Seventy Six Trombones	Book 2, page 43

ISBN 978-0-634-01853-4

HAL•LEONARD®
CORPORATION
7777 W. BLUEMOUND RD. P.O. BOX 13819 MILWAUKEE, WI 53213

Visit Hal Leonard Online at
www.halleonard.com

00868040

From THE SOUND OF MUSIC
EDELWEISS

VIOLIN
Solo

Lyrics by OSCAR HAMMERSTEIN II
Music by RICHARD RODGERS
Arranged by LLOYD CONLEY

From Walt Disney's BEAUTY AND THE BEAST: THE BROADWAY MUSICAL

BEAUTY AND THE BEAST

VIOLIN
Solo

Lyrics by HOWARD ASHMAN
Music by ALAN MENKEN
Arranged by LLOYD CONLEY

Disney Presents THE LION KING: THE BROADWAY MUSICAL

CIRCLE OF LIFE

VIOLIN
Solo

Music by ELTON JOHN
Lyrics by TIM RICE
Arranged by LLOYD CONLEY

00868040

From LES MISÉRABLES

I DREAMED A DREAM

VIOLIN
Solo

Music by CLAUDE-MICHEL SCHÖNBERG
Lyrics by ALAIN BOUBLIL,
JEAN-MARC NATEL and HERBERT KRETZMER
Arranged by LLOYD CONLEY

00868040

THE PHANTOM OF THE OPERA

VIOLIN
Solo

Music by **ANDREW LLOYD WEBBER**
Lyrics by **CHARLES HART**
Additional Lyrics by **RICHARD STILGOE** and **MIKE BATT**
Arranged by **LLOYD CONLEY**

00868040

From MISS SAIGON

SUN AND MOON

VIOLIN
Solo

Music by CLAUDE-MICHEL SCHÖNBERG
Lyrics by ALAIN BOUBLIL and RICHARD MALTBY JR.
Additional Lyrics by MICHAEL MAHLER
Adapted from original French Lyrics by ALAIN BOUBLIL
Arranged by LLOYD CONLEY

00868040

From the Musical CABARET
CABARET

VIOLIN
Solo

Words by FRED EBB
Music by JOHN KANDER
Arranged by LLOYD CONLEY

00868040

From MY FAIR LADY

GET ME TO THE CHURCH ON TIME

VIOLIN
Solo

Words by ALAN JAY LERNER
Music by FREDERICK LOEWE
Arranged by LLOYD CONLEY

00868040

From JOSEPH AND THE AMAZING TECHNICOLOR DREAMCOAT

GO GO GO JOSEPH

VIOLIN
Solo

Music by ANDREW LLOYD WEBBER
Lyrics by TIM RICE
Arranged by LLOYD CONLEY

From CATS
MEMORY

VIOLIN
Solo

Music by ANDREW LLOYD WEBBER
Text by TREVOR NUNN after T.S. ELIOT
Arranged by LLOYD CONLEY

From Meredith Willson's THE MUSIC MAN

SEVENTY SIX TROMBONES

VIOLIN
Solo

By MEREDITH WILLSON
Arranged by LLOYD CONLEY

00868040

From THE SOUND OF MUSIC
EDELWEISS

VIOLIN 1
String Orchestra Arrangement

Lyrics by OSCAR HAMMERSTEIN II
Music by RICHARD RODGERS
Arranged by LLOYD CONLEY

00868040

From THE SOUND OF MUSIC
EDELWEISS

VIOLIN 2
String Orchestra Arrangement

Lyrics by OSCAR HAMMERSTEIN II
Music by RICHARD RODGERS
Arranged by LLOYD CONLEY

From Walt Disney's BEAUTY AND THE BEAST: THE BROADWAY MUSICAL

BEAUTY AND THE BEAST

VIOLIN 1
String Orchestra Arrangement

Lyrics by HOWARD ASHMAN
Music by ALAN MENKEN
Arranged by LLOYD CONLEY

rit. opt.

From Walt Disney's BEAUTY AND THE BEAST: THE BROADWAY MUSICAL

BEAUTY AND THE BEAST

VIOLIN 2
String Orchestra Arrangement

Lyrics by HOWARD ASHMAN
Music by ALAN MENKEN
Arranged by LLOYD CONLEY

Disney Presents THE LION KING: THE BROADWAY MUSICAL

CIRCLE OF LIFE

VIOLIN 1
String Orchestra Arrangement

Music by ELTON JOHN
Lyrics by TIM RICE
Arranged by LLOYD CONLEY

00868040

CIRCLE OF LIFE

VIOLIN 2
String Orchestra Arrangement

Music by ELTON JOHN
Lyrics by TIM RICE
Arranged by LLOYD CONLEY

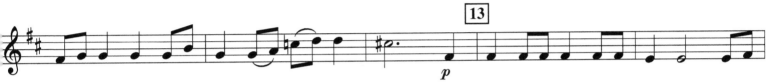

00868040

I DREAMED A DREAM

VIOLIN 1
String Orchestra Arrangement

Music by CLAUDE-MICHEL SCHÖNBERG
Lyrics by ALAIN BOUBLIL
JEAN-MARC NATEL and HERBERT KRETZMER
Arranged by LLOYD CONLEY

From LES MISÉRABLES

I DREAMED A DREAM

Violin 2
String Orchestra Arrangement

Music by CLAUDE-MICHEL SCHÖNBERG
Lyrics by ALAIN BOUBLIL,
JEAN-MARC NATEL and HERBERT KRETZMER
Arranged by LLOYD CONLEY

00868040

From THE PHANTOM OF THE OPERA

THE PHANTOM OF THE OPERA

VIOLIN 1
String Orchestra Arrangement

Music by ANDREW LLOYD WEBBER
Lyrics by CHARLES HART
Additional Lyrics by RICHARD STILGOE and MIKE BATT
Arranged by LLOYD CONLEY

00868040

THE PHANTOM OF THE OPERA

VIOLIN 2
String Orchestra Arrangement

Music by ANDREW LLOYD WEBBER
Lyrics by CHARLES HART
Additional Lyrics by RICHARD STILGOE and MIKE BATT
Arranged by LLOYD CONLEY

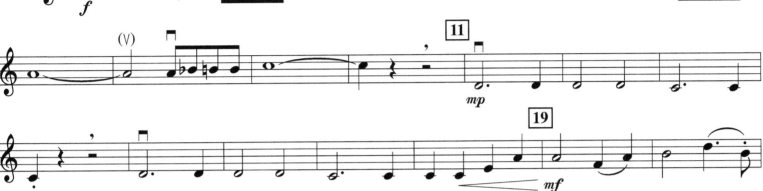

From MISS SAIGON
SUN AND MOON

Violin 1
String Orchestra Arrangement

Music by CLAUDE-MICHEL SCHÖNBERG
Lyrics by ALAIN BOUBLIL and RICHARD MALTBY JR
Additional Lyrics by MICHAEL MAHLER
Adapted from original French Lyrics by ALAIN BOUBLIL
Arranged by LLOYD CONLEY

SUN AND MOON

Music by CLAUDE-MICHEL SCHÖNBERG
Lyrics by ALAIN BOUBLIL and RICHARD MALTBY JR.
Additional Lyrics by MICHAEL MAHLER
Adapted from original French Lyrics by ALAIN BOUBLIL
Arranged by LLOYD CONLEY

Violin 2
String Orchestra Arrangement

00868039

From the Musical CABARET

CABARET

Violin 1
String Orchestra Arrangement

Words by FRED EBB
Music by JOHN KANDER
Arranged by LLOYD CONLEY

From the Musical CABARET
CABARET

VIOLIN 2
String Orchestra Arrangement

Words by FRED EBB
Music by JOHN KANDER
Arranged by LLOYD CONLEY

00868040

From MY FAIR LADY

Get Me to the Church on Time

VIOLIN 1
String Orchestra Arrangement

Words by ALAN JAY LERNER
Music by FREDERICK LOEWE
Arranged by LLOYD CONLEY

Get Me to the Church on Time

Violin 2
String Orchestra Arrangement

Words by ALAN JAY LERNER
Music by FREDERICK LOEWE
Arranged by LLOYD CONLEY

00868040

From JOSEPH AND THE AMAZING TECHNICOLOR DREAMCOAT

GO GO GO JOSEPH

VIOLIN 1
String Orchestra Arrangement

Music by ANDREW LLOYD WEBBER
Lyrics by TIM RICE
Arranged by LLOYD CONLEY

From **JOSEPH AND THE AMAZING TECHNICOLOR DREAMCOAT**
GO GO GO JOSEPH

Violin 2
String Orchestra Arrangement

Music by **ANDREW LLOYD WEBBER**
Lyrics by **TIM RICE**
Arranged by **LLOYD CONLEY**

00868040

From CATS
MEMORY

VIOLIN 1
String Orchestra Arrangement

Music by ANDREW LLOYD WEBBER
Text by TREVOR NUNN after T.S. ELIOT
Arranged by LLOYD CONLEY

From CATS
MEMORY

VIOLIN 2
String Orchestra Arrangement

Music by ANDREW LLOYD WEBBER
Text by TREVOR NUNN after T.S. ELIOT
Arranged by LLOYD CONLEY

From Meredith Willson's THE MUSIC MAN

SEVENTY SIX TROMBONES

VIOLIN 1
String Orchestra Arrangement

By MEREDITH WILLSON
Arranged by LLOYD CONLEY

From Meredith Willson's THE MUSIC MAN

SEVENTY SIX TROMBONES

By MEREDITH WILLSON
Arranged by LLOYD CONLEY

OLIN 2
ring Orchestra Arrangement

68040